I REALLY REALLY REALLY WANT ANSWERS ABOUT NOAH!

Ruth Carter

1:1 Answers
IN GENESIS™

Ark Encounter, Williamstown, KY

Ark Encounter, Williamstown

Ark Encounter, Williamstown, KY

Dedication

This book is dedicated to my dear father and mother, Ed and Nellie Schuit, who are now with the Lord. They taught me that Jesus is my Ark of safety. Because of your training, I will see you again, Mom and Dad. Can't wait!

I wish to give special thanks for:

Jesus, my Savior, whose sacrifice on the cross saved me from the punishment my sins deserve.

All the helpers from inside and outside Answers in Genesis who run my computer, display my props, lead small groups, and prepare the crafts for the Answers 4 Kids workshops. This book was written for our students.

T.F. Marsh and Diane King, whose art and design work are simply an extension of my written words. You read my mind. You make it flow. You put up with my idiosyncrasies! Thank you!

My good husband, Steve, who encourages when I am discouraged, brainstorms when my ideas dry up, and goes to bat for me when doors seem closed. He's the greatest partner in the process!

The thunder was crashing.
The lightning was snapping.
It was the worst of all storms of the sea.
The rain kept on pounding.
The water kept on rising.
Why, oh my, why , must this be?

Plants were uprooted.
Trees were demolished.
Sea creatures died under debris.
Air-breathing land animals,
Yes, even people,
Were drowned in the
depths of the sea.

So what was the reason
For this severe action?
Why should a storm like this be?
It was epic, catastrophic, once-in-a lifetime,
A happening few could foresee!
The Bible, our history book,
has all the answers.
Let's go there to get a good start.
What was the purpose?
Please give me the details,
Of the storm that tore earth apart.

THE PURPOSE

When God first created our world, it was perfect. There was no disease. There was no pain. There was no suffering. There was no death. And in that perfect world, God created the first man and the first woman, Adam and Eve. He told them to take care of their garden home. He gave them permission to eat the fruit of the trees for their food. There was just one "do-not-do" garden rule God commanded them to obey. They were never to eat the fruit from the tree of the knowledge of good and evil or they would surely die. Adam and Eve knew what God said and obeyed for a time.

Creation Museum, Petersburg, KY

Creation Museum, Petersburg, KY

But God has an enemy who was active even back then. His name is Satan. One day Satan spoke out of the mouth of a snake and tricked Eve into eating the forbidden fruit. She thought it would make her wise. She thought she would become like God, but just the opposite happened. She took a bite and gave the fruit to her husband to eat. In the moment they did, all of world history changed because sin entered the perfect garden home. Sin is anything we say or think or do that disobeys God.

Sin always has consequences, and one result of Adam and Eve's disobedience was that they had to leave their garden home. Their sin had ruined the perfect world God created. Another consequence was that everyone born into the human race since that time has been born with a sin problem that separates them from God.

Creation Museum, Petersburg, KY

Adam and Eve had children and grandchildren and great grandchildren and great, great grandchildren, and all of these were born with sinful hearts. Soon, the whole world was filled with people whose thoughts and behavior were totally wicked.

How many people were on the earth at the time of the Flood?

Because people lived very long ages and had lots of kids, it is possible that there were hundreds of millions of people living at this time.

I don't know what you would have done,
If your perfect world got ruined by sin.
But I know that God sent a most remarkable event.

THE PERSON

Sometime after Noah turned 500 years old, God called him. We know that Noah lived a total of 950 years, so this was just halfway through his lifetime. Noah was a father of three sons. He was probably a strong and very intelligent man. The Bible says "Noah was a just man, perfect in his generations". It says he "walked with God." The New Testament calls Noah a "preacher of righteousness." I think he was a good choice for the assignment God was about to give him, don't you?

The PURPOSE was clear.
The PERSON was ready.
God next shared His PLAN,
That would be so vast and deadly.

Noah in his study displayed in the Ark Encounter

THE PLAN

God told Noah "I myself am going to send floodwaters on this earth to destroy every living thing that breathes. Everything on earth will die. You are to build a large Ark." Then God added "You and your wife and your sons and their wives will all enter the Ark. You will also take aboard a male and female of every kind of animal, seven pairs of every kind of flying creature, and two of every kind of animal that scurries along the ground. Bring seven pairs of the clean animals you will use for sacrifices, like cows, sheep, goats and rams. Oh, and Noah, be sure to take on board enough food for your family and all the animals."

This sounded like a HUGE, IMPOSSIBLE assignment, but do you know what we read? "Noah did everything exactly as God had commanded him!"

What was an ark?

An ark was a container used to preserve life. It was not a ship that needed an engine to get from one place to another. It was a large, long boat whose job was simply to float and keep its cargo safe.

The PURPOSE was clear.
The PERSON was in place.
God shared His great PLAN,
To judge the human race.
An Ark would be built.
God had specifics in mind.
So next came the PREPARATION,
That would spare mankind.

PREPARATION

These are the directions God gave Noah for building the Ark:

- Take gopherwood.

- Make the whole Ark 300 cubits long, 50 cubits wide, and 30 cubits high (510 feet long, 85 feet wide, and 51 feet high).

- Make three decks.

- Put an opening below the roof.

- Build a door in the side.

- Put rooms in the Ark.

- Paint the Ark inside and out with "pitch."

And what do you think Noah did? "Noah did everything exactly as God had commanded him."

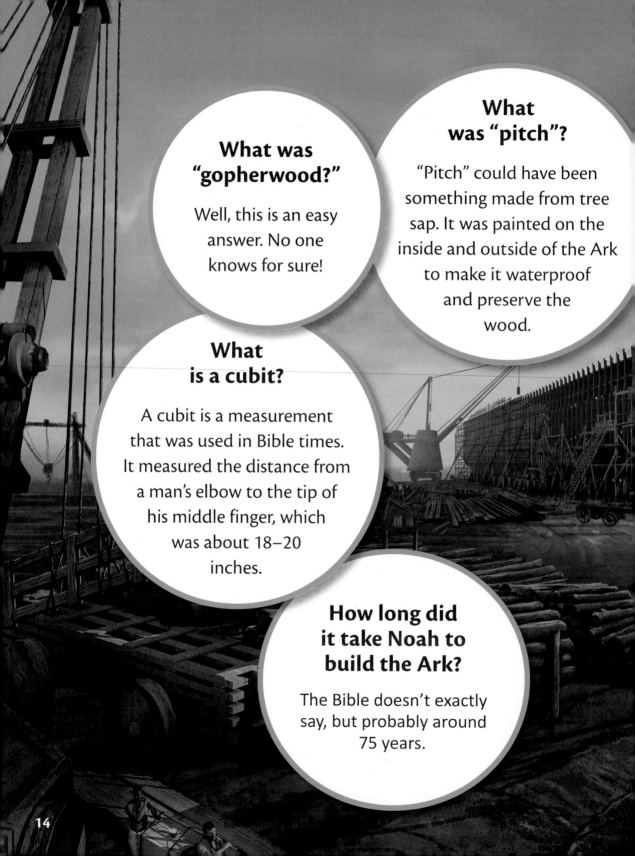

What was "gopherwood?"

Well, this is an easy answer. No one knows for sure!

What was "pitch"?

"Pitch" could have been something made from tree sap. It was painted on the inside and outside of the Ark to make it waterproof and preserve the wood.

What is a cubit?

A cubit is a measurement that was used in Bible times. It measured the distance from a man's elbow to the tip of his middle finger, which was about 18–20 inches.

How long did it take Noah to build the Ark?

The Bible doesn't exactly say, but probably around 75 years.

With the PURPOSE,
the PERSON, the PLAN,
and PREPARATION,
Noah was the focus of this
amazing operation.
But now things would change.
Miracles would happen.
It would become God's "show time"
For Noah, his wife, and children.

GOD'S SHOW TIME

Noah and his family went on board the Ark. The first miracle God performed is that He gathered the land animals. God brought a pair of every unclean animal and seven pairs of every flying creature and clean animal to Noah. There were wild animals and tame animals, large animals and small animals, furry animals and scaly animals, slithery animals and creeping animals, and every kind of bird. The animal parade was truly God's show time!

What is an animal kind?

An animal kind is a grouping of different animals that can have babies together. Noah took aboard a male and female of every animal kind, not two of every animal. So, for example, Noah could have taken two wolf-like dogs, but not two poodles, and two cocker spaniels, and two collies. From the two wolf-like dogs could have come all the varieties of dogs after the Flood

The cattle kind displayed in the Ark Encounter

By taking representatives of animal kinds, there were far fewer animals on the Ark than you might expect. These early animal kinds might have looked pretty strange, but from them came all the animals we know today. Creation scientists think there were fewer than 7,000 animals total on the Ark, which represents about 1,400 different animal kinds.

Were sea creatures on the Ark?

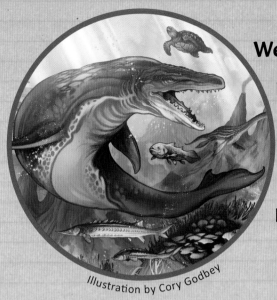

No, when God gave the list of animals that Noah was to include, sea creatures were not mentioned. God knew enough of them would survive the Flood since their natural home is in water.

Illustration by Cory Godbey

Were dinosaurs on the Ark?

Absolutely! There were about 60–90 different kinds of dinosaurs living on the earth before the Flood. God said take two of each kind of air-breathing, land animal. That included dinosaur kinds, so that's what Noah did.

Was there enough room on the Ark for all these animals?

Oh my, this Ark was huge! It could carry the same load as about 450 semi-trailers! Experts say that the animals could have occupied less than half the space in the Ark, leaving plenty of room for food.

The rebbachisaur kind displayed in the Ark Encounter

The second place where a miracle was seen was that God was in charge of the door. The timing of this water catastrophe was totally under God's control. It appears that God gave Noah seven days to load up the animals that had gathered, and then He shut the door as the catastrophe was ready to begin.

God shut the door!

God started the Flood
in two different ways,
One was familiar,
the other unknown today.
The "fountains of the great
deep broke open," we're told.
Then buckets of rain fell!
What a thing to behold!

Puddles grew to ponds.
Ponds grew to lakes.
Lakes grew to rivers flowing
wildly . . . goodness sakes.
Before they knew it, the Ark was afloat,
And everything drowned that
was not on the boat.
It was a horrible happening
of unimaginable proportion!
It was a water catastrophe that
caused worldwide destruction!

THE FLOOD

God's judgment on the people demonstrated that their sin was severe. It happened more than 4,000 years ago. The Bible states that first the "fountains of the great deep broke open." Scientists explain that the crust of our earth is made up of large plates which shift and move. These plate movements cause earthquakes and volcanoes and tsunamis. Yes, somehow the Flood started when the earth's crust broke open, allowing water to gush out from below. What was once one huge landmass was broken apart into smaller pieces that moved rapidly across the earth's surface.

Then rain poured from the sky for forty days and forty nights. The water rose and began to collect rapidly, sweeping across the land. Deep, rushing water is very, very powerful. It uprooted growing things, tore apart the land, drowned all land animals that needed air to breathe, pushed along tons and tons of sediment, and quickly buried many plants and animals under wet sand and mud. As it continued to rain, the water devastated the entire earth! At its deepest point the global ocean was more than 20 feet over the tallest mountain back then. But during all this time, Noah, his family, and the animal cargo were safe inside the Ark. At the end of 150 days, the waters began to retreat.

Water, water everywhere.
When would this huge storm stop?
Again it took God's power
To declare "not one more drop."
God sent a wind to blow and dry
A very soggy land.
And finally five months from the start,
The Ark landed at God's command.

Illustration by Paul Agner

THE LANDING

The Bible says the Ark came to rest on the mountains of Ararat. These mountains exist today in eastern Turkey. Noah and his family were probably very anxious to step onto dry land again, but they had to be patient.

About nine months after the Flood began, Noah conducted a bird experiment to figure out how dry the earth was getting to be. The raven's turn was first. A raven is a strong scavenger, and Noah let it out through the window he had made in the Ark. The raven flew back and forth as it explored the land that was starting to appear and dry out.

Next, Noah released a smaller, gentler bird. It was a dove. Back and forth it flew, but it could not find a clean, dry place to land. Noah

brought it back inside to rest. He waited another week and sent out the dove a second time. The bird flew back and forth and returned that evening with a fresh olive leaf in its beak.

Noah was happy to see that the trees had started growing, and the floodwaters were almost gone. He waited another week and sent out the dove again. This time it never came back.

A couple of months later, God instructed them to leave the Ark: Noah, his wife, his sons, and their wives, and all the animals. God was pleased that the first thing Noah did was to build an altar where he offered sacrifices to thank God for His faithful care. After one entire year, Noah and his family had made it safely through the greatest storm in the history of the world!

The PURPOSE, the PERSON, the PLAN, and PREPARATION Put God's judgment for sin on wide display. Then God closed the event with a wonderful PROMISE: Never again would a flood be the means to repay the evil and wickedness of human behavior. A rainbow sealed God's promise. It's a reminder today.

Illustration by Paul Agner

HAS NOAH'S ARK EVER BEEN FOUND?

There have been many attempts to find Noah's Ark, but none have been successful. Eastern Turkey is a difficult place to explore. It is likely that the Ark no longer exists. It could have been destroyed due to harsh weather or activity from volcanoes that were present after the Flood. Noah and his family may have used the wood to build their homes when they got off the Ark. These are just guesses. No one really knows the answer.

The Ahora Gorge from 11,000 feet elevation.

The Ahora Gorge, deeper than Grand Canyon, swallows climbers.

Climbing along steep ridge line loose glacial skre

Photos by Dr. John Morris

So we've talked about the PURPOSE,
the PERSON, and the PLAN,
The PREPARATIONS, the
PROMISE that God gave to man
But wait, there is a PROBLEM
people talk about today.
They claim it didn't happen
as the Bible does say.
They think the Flood was
small, a mere local event.

They don't believe God's written
Word. It's their argument.
So what is your answer when friends
question the big Flood?
Can you show them that the WHOLE
WORLD was covered
By all this rain and mud?
Read on for information that you can
share with your close friends.
The Bible is completely true.
The evidence never ends.

EVIDENCES TODAY FOR A WORLDWIDE FLOOD

Fossils found all over the world

If the Flood of Noah really did cover the whole earth as the Bible describes, we should find billions of fossils (dead creatures turned to stone) over all the world's continents. And that is exactly what is found. Fossils are found on the highest mountains. Fossils are found in the middle of continents where there is no water present today. Fossils are found in the cliffs at the seashore. During the worldwide Flood of Noah, the conditions were perfect for fossils to be made. The worldwide discovery of fossils would not occur if the Flood was just a local event.

Amudei Shelomo in Timna, Israel.

Tapeats sandstone in the Grand Canyon, AZ.

The Grand Canyon has a unique sandstone known as the Tapeats Sandstone. Other regions have the same basic sandstone, which always appears at the bottom of the stack of sedimentary layers.

Photos by
Dr. Andrew Snelling

Vast layers of sedimentary rock

Sedimentary rock is rock laid down by water. If Noah's Flood covered the whole earth, we should see layers of sedimentary rock extending great distances across the continents in our world today, shouldn't we? And that is exactly what we find. This would not be found if the Flood were just a local event on one continent.

27

MEXICO

AFRICA

Norse

Greek

Pawnee

Aztec

Mayan

Flood legends in countries around the world

If the Flood of Noah destroyed the whole world, and only Noah and his family survived, don't you think stories about such a huge catastrophe would have been passed down to the later generations who descended from Noah? And that is exactly what we find. In fact, there are at least 200 stories about a worldwide Flood from cultures all over the world. These would not be found if the Flood was just a local event.

As we come to the close
Of an interesting look
At the world's greatest storm
From the world's greatest book,
Two lessons emerge
For our minds to consider:
One is sad news, and one
is so much better!

legend illustrations by Jon Seest

THE GLAD NEWS

But the good news is that God is love!
He gives us a fresh start.
And just as the Ark saved people from the Flood
So Jesus saves a sin–filled heart.
The Ark had one door. There was only one way
To escape God's punishment for sin.
Jesus is our door. He is the only way
For our heart to be clean and forgiven.

That is the
hopeful, awesome,
marvelous, incredible,
life-changing message from
the worldwide Flood of Noah!

ABOUT THE AUTHOR

Ruth Carter
is a writer and presenter
of kids' workshops at the
Creation Museum. She is
a mom of four sons and
lives in northern Kentucky
with her husband.

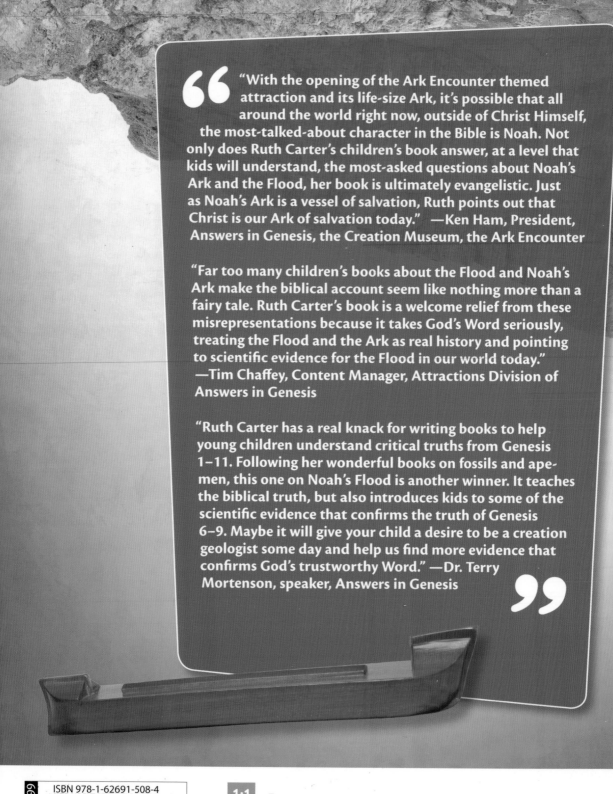

"With the opening of the Ark Encounter themed attraction and its life-size Ark, it's possible that all around the world right now, outside of Christ Himself, the most-talked-about character in the Bible is Noah. Not only does Ruth Carter's children's book answer, at a level that kids will understand, the most-asked questions about Noah's Ark and the Flood, her book is ultimately evangelistic. Just as Noah's Ark is a vessel of salvation, Ruth points out that Christ is our Ark of salvation today." —Ken Ham, President, Answers in Genesis, the Creation Museum, the Ark Encounter

"Far too many children's books about the Flood and Noah's Ark make the biblical account seem like nothing more than a fairy tale. Ruth Carter's book is a welcome relief from these misrepresentations because it takes God's Word seriously, treating the Flood and the Ark as real history and pointing to scientific evidence for the Flood in our world today." —Tim Chaffey, Content Manager, Attractions Division of Answers in Genesis

"Ruth Carter has a real knack for writing books to help young children understand critical truths from Genesis 1–11. Following her wonderful books on fossils and ape-men, this one on Noah's Flood is another winner. It teaches the biblical truth, but also introduces kids to some of the scientific evidence that confirms the truth of Genesis 6–9. Maybe it will give your child a desire to be a creation geologist some day and help us find more evidence that confirms God's trustworthy Word." —Dr. Terry Mortenson, speaker, Answers in Genesis

U.S. $4.99

ISBN 978-1-62691-508-4

9 781626 915084

1:1 Answers IN GENESIS™

KidsAnswers.org